RENÉ-CHARLES
NYC

RENÉ-CHARLES

NYC

little bulldog in the big city

BY **RENÉ-CHARLES**

WITH **EVAN CUTTIC** AND **RYAN NALLS**

Running Press
PHILADELPHIA · LONDON

Books published by Running Press are available at special discounts for bulk purchases in the United States by corporations, institutions, and other organizations. For more information, please contact the Special Markets Department at the Perseus Books Group, 2300 Chestnut Street, Suite 200, Philadelphia, PA 19103, or call (800) 810-4145, ext. 5000, or e-mail special.markets@perseusbooks.com.

ISBN 978-0-7624-6001-4
Library of Congress Control Number: 2016943205

E-book ISBN 978-0-7624-6108-0

9 8 7 6 5 4 3 2 1
Digit on the right indicates the number of this printing

Cover and Interior design by Ashley Haag
Edited by Jennifer Kasius
Typography: Interstate

Running Press Book Publishers
2300 Chestnut Street
Philadelphia, PA 19103-4371

Visit us on the web!
www.runningpress.com

STEP INTO THE BIG APPLE, AND THE WORLD OF RENÉ-CHARLES,

Manhattan's most iconic French bulldog, who finds his life of popularity and privilege both overwhelming and exhausting. Boozy brunches, lunch-hour shopping sprees, dinner at the hottest new spots in town—René-Charles struts and snoozes his way through the city that never sleeps with confidence and New York attitude. For this snarky pup, life in the upper crust is much more about *who* you're wearing than *what* you're wearing. And if he doesn't like either, be prepared to hear about it. Because in the dog-eat-dog world of René-Charles, you can call your apartment a penthouse all you want, but if you're not at the very top, you might as well be in the lobby.

have you ever seen
Beyoncé holding her
own umbrella?

didn't think so.

maybe they keep
the luxury goods in the
"beyond" section.

can we go to
that restaurant
i like?

the one with
the really small
and expensive
portions.

no.

absolutely not.

when you said
"subway" i thought
you were talking about
sandwiches.

help!

i went to brooklyn
for brunch and i think
i caught the hipster!

in LA your
car matters.

in NY your
coat matters.

i think i'm going
to take a nap.

wake me up in 10 hours.

running so late
because i don't have
a rolex.

i'm not really hungry,
i split a dozen cronuts with
the trash earlier today.

can we pull over
at Saks?

jacqueline has
some items on
hold for me.

one of us is going to
have to change.

i don't often eat
off a silver platter.

usually it's gold
or platinum.

i can't sleep.

i'm haunted by
all of the things
i want to buy.

SWEAR
JAR

**it's going to be an
expensive day.**

does Barneys deliver?

hi,
i live next door.

can i borrow
a few cups of
vodka?

LET ME SEE WHO YOU'RE TEXTING.

it's going to take
more than a scarf to
make this look chic.

i wonder if that girl
is crying because of
her kitten heels.

ugh.

can you just pick one.

it's a tree
not a rolex.

over the river
and through the woods
to louis vuitton i go.

if you're planning
to serve me
wine from a box,
this will be a
very unhappy hour.

is this how they make
pumpkin spice?

just called out sick
for the fourth day in a row!

you will pay for this,

in the form of a bill from
my therapist.

just a single guy,
out here searching for my
Dr. Right.

every crosswalk
is a runway.

today is going to
be a struggle.

i only got,
like,
14 hours of sleep.

ugh.

i hate when i can't find
any of my cars.

chew louder.

you know i love that.

if i see one more
pair of uggs,
i'm going to lose it.

yep.

too much
champagne
again.

i've got
the spins.

i'm not sure that
you should pet me.

i'm not supposed to
trust anyone
with a fake chanel bag.

**exercising now
so that i have something to
complain about later.**

i pour
orange juice into
expensive champagne
and don't even feel
slightly bad
about it.

this party better
be good.

i'm not wasting
this outfit on your
basic friends.

**it's called fashion,
you clearly wouldn't understand.**

don't wake me up,
i'm working.

my fake smile.

if i still have morning breath it's because i slept all day.

i take back all of
the nasty things i've said
about Los Angeles.

i don't have a
spending problem,

you just have an
income problem.

ew.

cargo shorts.

get a life, morning people.

i'm going to need
all of it.

why is it always freezing in this office?

I AM BEYONCÉ,
YOU ARE MICHELLE!

does it look
like i care
that guacamole
costs extra?

because i don't.

there.

i decorated.

now give me gifts.

just chugged
a venti iced coffee!

what is this.

a bottle for ANTS?

**you can stay
but your outfit must go.**

babe,
can you hand me
another towel and
my wine glass?

it's not weird.

a lot of people
prefer to go camping at
the Four Seasons.

i'm just going to
hold on to this.

we don't need you texting
"you know who" tonight.

sometimes i make my staff
do the walking for me.

i don't speak french,

i speak trench.

i hate all liquids that don't contain at least 8% alcohol.

ugh.

i can't.

give me these.

if you won't venture
out in the snow
for a few bottles of wine,
i will.

honestly
don't start barking at me
until i've had my coffee.

i have such great taste in art.

i need this wind
like i need more kale.

it's not a fort,
it's a suite.

but you wouldn't
know that
since you've never
stayed in one.

i need advil and fried food.

now.

this hat keeps
my ears warm
and also shields me
from your nagging.

having a bad ear day.

it just doesn't feel like
a good workout class
unless i've paid at least $40.

pro tip:

girls dig guys in scarves.

laughing because
i'm pretty sure i spend
your entire salary on
starbucks and sushi alone.

on wednesdays,
we wear pink.

i'm not going to
work today.

i have a zit.

not sure which
hurts my ears more,
the car horns,
the construction,
or the screech of your voice.

i can't hang out tonight.

i already have plans.

sometimes

i wish you were a pizza.

did i wash it all off?

the nachos
and regret
from the weekend?

i'm still awake.

just resting my eyes.

i'm ready for bed
because
i never got dressed today.

no.

the only hydrants
that i do business with
are in front of
five-star hotels.

it's so hard waking up at
the break of noon.

i bet you
pronounce espresso
"EXPRESS-o."

hi.

yep.

those are crocs.

in public.

i'm not exactly religious,
but sometimes in the park
i do pray for luxury goods
and opportunities to
criticize others.

daily goal:

**get from my apartment
to the lobby
without having to talk to
any of my creepy neighbors.**

reasons to love
the color green:

money,

guacamole,

and me in this coat.

life is short.

just buy it.

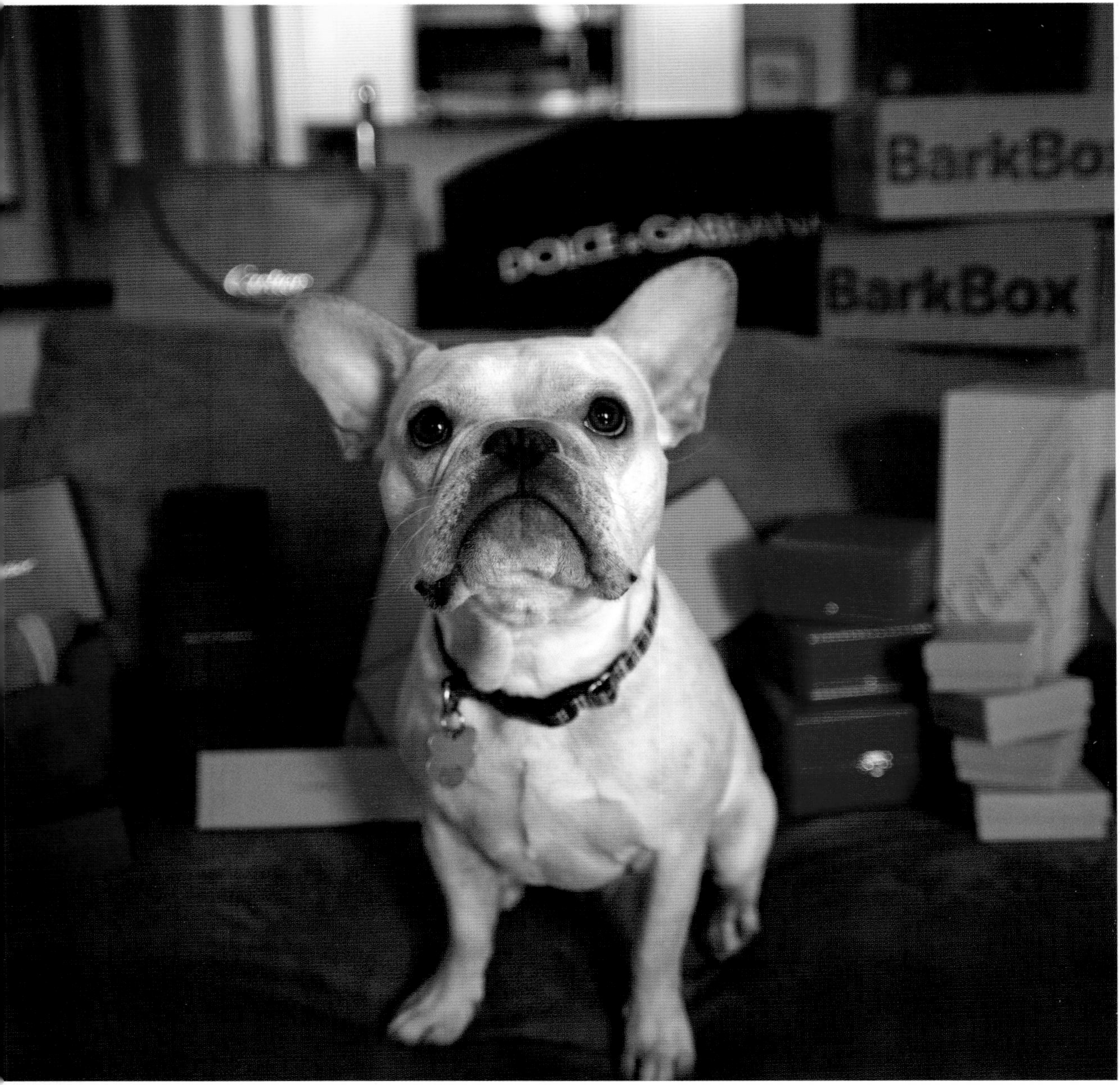
BarkBox
BarkBox

sigh.

another
tinder date
disaster.

ACKNOWLEDGMENTS

René-Charles would like to offer special thanks to his dear friends and personal mentors (in order of net worth): Oprah Winfrey, Beyoncé, Céline Dion, Gisele Bündchen, Martha Stewart, Roger Federer, Ina Garten, Kris Jenner, Khloé Kardashian, and Barack and Michelle Obama.

ABOUT THE AUTHORS

EVAN CUTTIC and **RYAN NALLS** are the humans behind the popular Instagram account @ReneCharlesNYC. They're also René-Charles's overworked and underpaid personal assistants, photographers, valets, and parents.

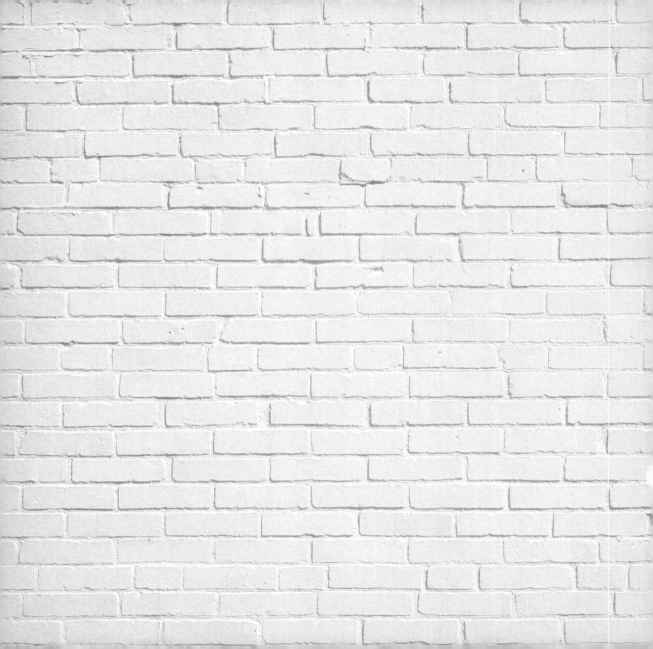